Virginia

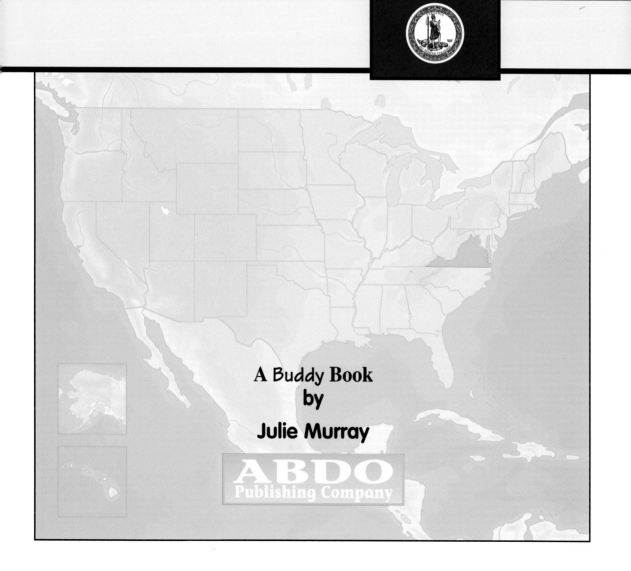

A Buddy Book
by
Julie Murray

ABDO
Publishing Company

VISIT US AT
www.abdopub.com

Published by ABDO Publishing Company, 4940 Viking Drive, Edina, Minnesota 55435.

Printed in the United States.

Edited by: Sarah Tieck
Contributing Editor: Michael P. Goecke
Graphic Design: Deb Coldiron, Maria Hosley
Image Research: Sarah Tieck
Photographs: Clipart.com, Eyewire, Library of Congress, Medio, One Mile Up, Photodisc, Photos.com, U.S. Dept of Defense, Virginia Beach Tourism

Library of Congress Cataloging-in-Publication Data

Murray, Julie, 1969-
  Virginia / Julie Murray.
      p. cm. — (The United States)
  Includes index.
    Contents: A snapshot of Virginia — Where is Virginia? — All about Virginia — Cities and the capital — Famous citizens — Virginia's landscape — Colonial Williamsurg — The Pentagon — A history of Virginia.
    ISBN 1-59197-705-3
      1. Virginia—Juvenile literature. I. Title.

F226.3.M87 2005
975.5—dc22
                                                2005048085

Table Of Contents

A Snapshot Of Virginia

Virginia is known for its history. Virginia was one of the 13 original colonies. Virginia fought for freedom from England. Even this state's name is historic. It comes from Queen Elizabeth I of England. She was called the "Virgin Queen."

Queen Elizabeth I of England

There are 50 states in the United States. Every state is different. Every state has an official nickname. Virginia's nickname is "Old Dominion." King Charles II of England gave Virginia this name. It refers to the state's loyalty during an English war in the mid-1600s.

Virginia became the 10th state on June 25, 1788. Virginia is the 36th-largest state. It has 40,598 square miles (105,148 sq km) of land. It is home to 7,078,515 people.

Where Is Virginia?

There are four parts of the United States. Each part is called a region. Each region is in a different area of the country. The United States Census Bureau says the four regions are the Northeast, the South, the Midwest, and the West.

Virginia is located in the South region of the United States. In general, Virginia's weather is mild. Summers are hot and humid. Some parts of the state, like the mountains, are cooler. They even get snow.

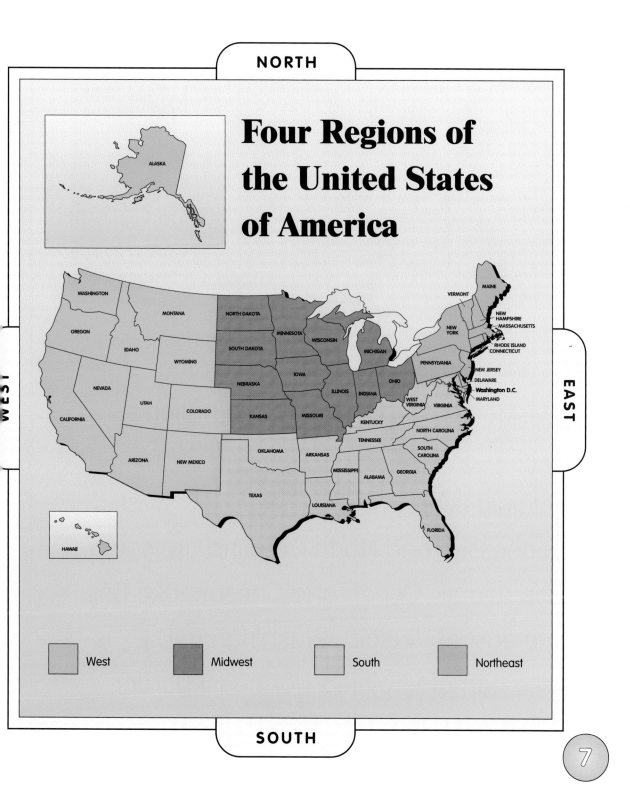

Four Regions of the United States of America

ALASKA

WASHINGTON
MONTANA
NORTH DAKOTA
MINNESOTA
VERMONT
MAINE
OREGON
IDAHO
WYOMING
SOUTH DAKOTA
WISCONSIN
MICHIGAN
NEW YORK
NEW HAMPSHIRE
MASSACHUSETTS
RHODE ISLAND
CONNECTICUT
NEVADA
UTAH
COLORADO
NEBRASKA
IOWA
ILLINOIS
INDIANA
OHIO
PENNSYLVANIA
NEW JERSEY
DELAWARE
Washington D.C.
MARYLAND
CALIFORNIA
KANSAS
MISSOURI
WEST VIRGINIA
VIRGINIA
KENTUCKY
NORTH CAROLINA
ARIZONA
NEW MEXICO
OKLAHOMA
ARKANSAS
TENNESSEE
SOUTH CAROLINA
MISSISSIPPI
ALABAMA
GEORGIA
TEXAS
LOUISIANA
FLORIDA

HAWAII

West
Midwest
South
Northeast

The White House is in Washington, D.C.
It is near Virginia's border.

Virginia is bordered by five other states, two bodies of water, and the nation's capital. Maryland is northeast. West Virginia is northwest. Kentucky is west. Tennessee and North Carolina are south. The Atlantic Ocean and Chesapeake Bay are east of Virginia. Washington, D.C., is also part of Virginia's northeast border.

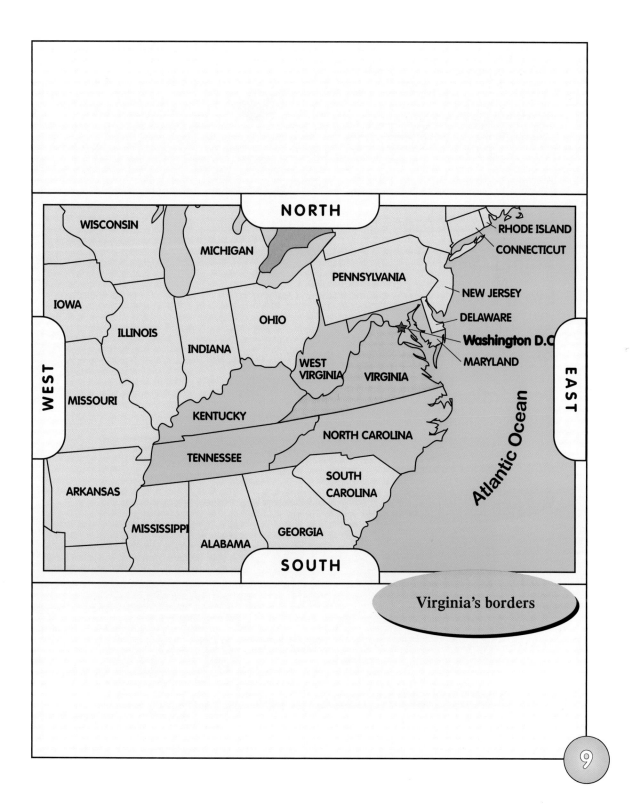

Virginia's borders

Virginia

State abbreviation: **VA**

State nickname: Old Dominion

State capital: Richmond

State motto: *Sic semper tyrannis* ("Thus Always to Tyrants")

Statehood: June 25, 1788, 10th state

Population: 7,078,515, ranks 12th

State flag:
Adopted in 1861

Land area: 40,598 square miles (105,148 sq km), ranks 36th

State tree: Flowering dogwood

State song: No official state song

State government: Three branches: legislative, executive, and judicial

Average July temperature: 75°F (24°C)

Average January temperature: 36°F (2°C)

State flower:
Flowering dogwood

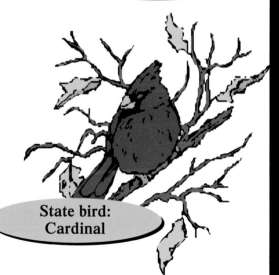

State bird:
Cardinal

State dog:
American foxhound

Cities And The Capital

Richmond is the capital of Virginia. The James River goes through the middle of this city.

There is a famous statue of George Washington in the Capitol. Jean Antoine Houdon made the sculpture. The sculpture is famous because George Washington posed for it when he was alive.

The Virginia State Capitol

People bike and walk along the boardwalk in Virginia Beach.

Virginia Beach is the largest city in the state. It is located along the Atlantic Ocean in southeast Virginia. It is also near Chesapeake Bay. Many people visit Virginia Beach for vacations. There are many miles of sandy beaches there. Also, there is a boardwalk where people shop, walk, and bike.

Famous Citizens

George Washington (1732–1799)

George Washington was born in Virginia. He led American soldiers in the American Revolutionary War. With his help, America became a new nation.

Washington served as president from 1789 to 1797. He helped to build a government that still exists today. Americans know George Washington as the "Father of the Country."

George Washington

Famous Citizens

Thomas Jefferson (1743–1826)

Thomas Jefferson was born in Virginia. He wrote the Declaration of Independence. His words: "All men are created equal," are famous. In 1801, Thomas Jefferson became the third president of the United States. Jefferson arranged for the United States to buy a piece of land west of the Mississippi River. This was known as the Louisiana Purchase. Later, he helped build the University of Virginia.

Thomas Jefferson

Dismal Swamp

The Dismal Swamp is in southeastern Virginia. This is one of the largest swamps in the United States. It covers about 750 square miles (2,000 sq km) of land in both Virginia and North Carolina.

This swamp has been around for thousands of years. In 1973, part of the swamp became a national wildlife refuge. This area is known as the Great Dismal Swamp National Wildlife Refuge.

This swamp has many different types of plants. There are vines hanging down. And, there are many different trees. These include red maple, pine, and Atlantic white cedar.

There are many hanging vines like this one in the Dismal Swamp.

A view of a swampy area in Virginia.

Swamps are damp and watery. Because of this, plants turn into peat when they die. Peat is made when plants and grass decay and form a mass. When peat is dried, it can be used for fuel and for bedding for animals.

This area is home to many different animals, too. Some of the animals include opossums, gray foxes, bears, and white-tailed deer.

Colonial Williamsburg

Williamsburg was the capital of Virginia from 1699 to 1780. Today, Williamsburg is a modern city. But, people can still visit part of the old city. The old city is now like a museum. It is called Colonial Williamsburg. Colonial Williamsburg is located in the center of present-day Williamsburg.

The Governor's Palace is in
Colonial Williamsburg.

Many tourists visit Colonial Williamsburg. They go to see what Williamsburg looked like in the 1700s. There are around 500 public buildings. Homes, shops, and taverns have all been reconstructed and restored to look like they did more than 200 years ago.

In Colonial Williamsburg, people wear colonial clothes and ride in carriages.

Workers even dress in outfits to resemble the clothes worn during that time period. They demonstrate crafts and trades that were happening during that time in history.

The Pentagon

The United States Department of Defense is located in a building called the Pentagon. This building is located in Arlington. It is close to Washington, D.C.

A view of the Pentagon.

The Pentagon is a large complex.
It has five sides like a pentagon.

The Pentagon is one of the world's largest office buildings. About 24,000 people work there. The Pentagon has shops, restaurants, and a bank. There is a system that sends letters through tubes. There is even a television station and a place for helicopters to land.

Tragedy struck the Pentagon on September 11, 2001. Terrorists crashed a plane into the Pentagon. This destroyed a section of the building and killed almost 200 people. There were also terrorist attacks in New York City and Pennsylvania that day, too.

The Pentagon was damaged on September 11, 2001. This shows part of the damage.

Virginia

1607: Jamestown is the first English colony established in the United States.

1754: The French and Indian War begins. It will end in 1763.

1776: Thomas Jefferson writes the Declaration of Independence.

1788: Virginia becomes the 10th state on June 25.

1789: George Washington becomes the first president of the United States.

1861: Richmond becomes the capital of the Southern states during the American Civil War.

1863: The western part of Virginia becomes West Virginia.

Integrated classrooms include students of all races.

1959: Virginia schools begin to integrate. This means that students of all races go to the same schools.

1990: L. Douglas Wilder becomes the first African-American governor in the United States.

2001: Terrorists crash a plane into the Pentagon on September 11.

2004: Richmond hosts the 150th Virginia State Fair.

Cities In Virginia

Arlington
Alexandria

Shadwell

Richmond ★
Williamsburg

Roanoke

Newport News
Norfolk
Virginia Beach
Portsmouth

Important Words

American Civil War the United States war between the Northern and the Southern states.

American Revolutionary War America fought for freedom from Great Britain in this famous war.

capital a city where government leaders meet.

colony a settlement.

humid air that is damp or moist.

nickname a name that describes something special about a person or a place.

terrorist a person who uses terror and/or violence to achieve an objective.

Web Sites

To learn more about Virginia, visit ABDO Publishing Company on the World Wide Web. Web site links about Virginia are featured on our Book Links page. These links are routinely monitored and updated to provide the most current information available.

www.abdopub.com

Index